WHERE'S MY STUFF?

Samantha Moss with
Professional Teen Organizer
Lesley Schwartz

Illustrated by Michael Wertz

First published in 2007 by
Zest Books, an imprint of Orange Avenue Publishing
35 Stillman Street, Suite 121, San Francisco, CA 94107
www.zestbooks.net

Created and produced by Zest Books, San Francisco, CA
© 2007 by Orange Avenue Publishing LLC
Illustrations © 2007 by Michael Wertz

Text set in Minion; title text set in Neuland; accent text set in NeutraText

Library of Congress Control Number: 2006940258
ISBN-13: 978-0-9772660-5-0
ISBN-10: 0-9772660-5-2

CREDITS
EDITORIAL DIRECTOR: Karen Macklin
CREATIVE DIRECTOR: Hallie Warshaw
WRITER: Samantha Moss
PROFESSIONAL CONSULTANT: Lesley Schwartz
EDITOR: Karen Macklin
ILLUSTRATOR: Michael Wertz
GRAPHIC DESIGNERS: Cari McLaughlin and Lisa Martin
PRODUCTION ARTIST: Cari McLaughlin

Printed in China.
First printing, 2007
10 9 8 7 6 5 4 3 2 1

Every effort has been made to ensure that the information presented is accurate. Readers are strongly advised to read product labels, follow manufacturers' instructions, and heed warnings. The publisher disclaims any liability for injuries, losses, untoward results, or any other damages that may result from the use of the information in this book.

WHERE'S MY STUFF?

TABLE OF CONTENTS

(smile!)

Everybody knows about the "s" word.

You've got it. We've got it. In fact, everybody's got way too much of it. And nobody wants to deal with it. We're talking about **stuff.**

It's not your fault. When your parents grew up, they had notebooks and pencils. You have a notebook computer, digital files, hard copies, *and* notebooks and pencils. They had piano lessons once a week after school. You've got five extracurricular activities with five different types of uniforms and equipment. You've also got emails to return, a blog to update, music to download, not to mention homework to do. Sure, your parents had homework, too. But yours must be typed, formatted, spell-checked, and backed up on your external hard drive.

So, you're thinking: What's wrong with stuff? I like stuff. I LIVE for stuff. The problem, as you may have guessed, isn't really your stuff. The problem is what to do with it all.

ORGANIZE

Your life is full of friends, classes, activities, and other things you love, but it is lacking one very basic element: order. You can't find your wallet most days. And you can't even find the time to look for it. You keep doing things like locking yourself out of the house, leaving your basketball uniform in the car under your guitar case, and accidentally deleting your final term papers from your computer. On top of it all, your back aches from lugging around that over-stuffed hauling device otherwise known as a backpack.

For some people, organizing comes easily. But for most of us, it's a learned skill. This book will show you not only how to get organized at school, at home, and on the go, but also what being organized can do for your life. Think less stress, more time with friends, extra cash, and greater independence. Keeping your life in order will help you keep your head in order, too. And, as you already know, that is no small victory.

GETTING STARTED

GETTING STARTED

Every fall, the same thing happens. You show up for the first day of school with a perfect new binder and a notebook for every class. Your room is neat, your desk is clean, and your new fall clothes are hanging spotless and wrinkle-free in your closet. (Well, at least they're *in* your closet.) *This year*, you think, *I'm on it.*

Six weeks into the semester, your backpack is a disaster. You've lost track of which notebook was for what, your binder is somewhere under the bed, and your homework (when you've done it *and* you can find it) is all crumpled and sad. Soon, you can't find your cell phone, and there's a very sinister-looking pile of rumpled clothing creeping its way across the bedroom floor. Your intentions were good, but here you are, snagged again. What happened?

While it's easy to blame disorganization on outside factors, like lack of space and too much stuff, it's often our mind-sets that keep us stuck in disorder. And when we are stuck in disorder, it's not just our notebooks that suffer, but our overall quality of life. In this chapter, you'll learn the Top 5 Benefits of being organized, and what mental obstacles are preventing you from enjoying them. Once you understand why you're stuck in disorder, you can start on the path to getting unstuck—for good.

1 Why Bother?
Learn the Top 5 Benefits of getting organized

Getting organized is not just about finding your missing homework or placating your angry parents. It's about the quality of your life.

Sure, your initial goal might be to solve the problem of an out-of-control school notebook or an unclosable bedroom closet. And that's fine. But once you solve these problems, you'll realize that the payoff goes way beyond being able to find your homework or a clean pair of socks. When your whole setup works *for* you and not against you, life just goes more smoothly. To see what we mean, check out these **Top 5 Benefits** of getting organized.

Benefit #1: Score Bonus Time

So, if you had an extra hour every day to do whatever you wanted, how would you spend it? Getting organized is a good way to find out. A big chunk of every day gets lost to the never-ending search for stuff, like looking for that other soccer cleat, digging for a pen in your cookie-crumbed backpack, or chasing down the house keys. And that's not even counting the time you waste *worrying* about not being able to find your math homework, or *obsessing* over how to tell your best friend that you lost her favorite bracelet. Getting organized frees you from this frenzy, leaving you with more time for the luxurious things in life. Like sleep.

Benefit #2: Cash In

It pays to put your life in order. Literally. One side effect of being disorganized is that things get ruined or lost all the time. Books evaporate, headphones break, sunglasses get sat on, and cell phone chargers mysteriously disappear. Replacing it all can add up to serious cash — cash that you could otherwise spend on the new things you really want instead of duplicates of stuff you already had.

Benefit #3: Chill Out

Getting organized is a sweet escape from stress. As you may have noticed, being disorganized is a drain on your nervous system. If a typical day for you means being 20 minutes late to school (again), brainstorming an excuse for not doing your math homework (again), and then borrowing someone else's foul-smelling T-shirt for gym (because you forgot yours … again), you're bound to arrive home completely exhausted. Being surrounded by turmoil keeps your mind in permanent panic mode, with no chance to rest. But when life is in order, your head can relax for a change—and those chewed-up stumps on the ends of your fingers might actually turn into nails again.

Benefit #4: Stay Connected

Creating order can score you social points, too. When life is messy, it's easy to get so wrapped up in worry that there's no brain space left for friends, even when they're right in front of you. Accidental glitches in your schedule—like saying yes to a movie with Denise when you're supposed to be at Mike's house—can put serious stress on a friendship. Between that and the way disorganization causes conflicts with parents, living in chaos can be downright lonely. But when serenity rules, there's more time and energy for the people you care about—and when you're more relaxed, they're more relaxed, too.

Benefit #5: Be Independent

The more consistently organized you are, the more your parents will trust you. And no matter what your parents are like, it's a universal fact that earning their trust will mean earning the right to make more decisions for yourself. Short of hypnosis, the only way to gain their trust is to do what you say you'll do, when you say you'll do it. It's much easier to follow through on promises if you have reminders in place—like a planner that helps you show up on time to babysit the paper-eating two-year-old next door. If you know how to manage your own schedule, you end up with more independence, less checking in with parents, and—who knows?—maybe even a shot at test-driving that amazing convertible in the storeroom window. Maybe.

2 What's Your O.Q.?
Take our quiz to learn your Organizing Quotient

All of us have little personality quirks that shape the way we deal with life. But if you're disorganized, odds are that your quirks are working against you. Take this **Organizing Quotient** quiz to see what's keeping you tangled up in tornadoville.

Circle your answers to find out your organizing type—and how this book will help tame your tornado once and for all.

1. You have a physics test tomorrow, but you haven't studied yet because

A. you've spent the last hour cleaning out your desk and arranging everything at perfect 90-degree angles to get your space "study ready."

B. you can't stop thinking about the English paper you still have to write, the half-read history book on your desk, how badly your room needs to be cleaned, how many emails you have to return, and what you're going to wear tomorrow.

C. you've already committed to plans with three friends this afternoon and are scheduled to help choreograph the headlining act at the school's hip-hop jam this evening. You've got an available slot tonight between 11 and 11:30. (Unfortunately, you're supposed to be in bed at 10:45.)

D. you decided instead to start working on some blueprints for a mini NASA space station for the upcoming science fair.

2. The contents of your closet include

A. broken stuff that you refuse to take into a repair shop because, even though you don't have the time, you really want to fix it yourself.

B. … you have no idea. (It's too much to think about.)

C. anything and everything you can possibly imagine.

D. running clothes for last year's marathon—with all the tags still on them.

3. You are known to

A. write and rewrite an email until you get it just right—even if it means your reply arrives a month after you first received the email.

B. avoid cleaning your room. (There's just too much to do—where would you even begin?)

C. collect free stuff. And lots of it.

D. spend hours reading magazines about all the famous movie stars you plan to model your life after.

4. On a typical Saturday, you find yourself

A. late to tennis practice because you spent the whole morning perfecting your backhand.

B. unable to get out of bed because you feel so overwhelmed by how much you have to do.

C. booking a different activity for every free hour of your weekend, and then double-booking when you run out of time.

D. staying home to plan out the next five years of your life … even though, come to think of it, you don't even have plans for tonight.

5. If someone opens your binder, odds are they'll see

A. nothing. You haven't found the perfect system yet to organize your papers, so you just keep them in a heap near your bed.

B. tons of to-do lists with hardly anything to-done.

C. so much paper it's a miracle the binder's not breaking. Oh wait…it *is* breaking.

D. applications for Ivy League grad schools (even though you can't seem to pass high school biology).

OK, now see which letter you picked the most. Then read your organizing profile below, and see how this book can help.

Mostly As:

The All-or-Nothing (but generally Nothing) Perfectionist Procrastinator

You love nothing more than a job well done. In fact, you're so into doing things in just the right way, you avoid starting to get organized unless you have endless time and a perfect plan to do it. But while you're waiting for that to happen, you notice that stuff is piling up. Before you know it, a year has passed and you can no longer close your closet door or use that chair in the corner because it's so overloaded with stuff.

In these pages you'll discover a secret: Organization is not the same thing as perfection. Perfection is impossible. And even if it *were* possible, it'd be SO boring. Being organized, on the other hand, lets you live the way you want to, focusing on what matters to you most. It's strictly a quality-of-life equation: The more organized you are, the better things go. The next time you get stuck in that all-or-nothing state of mind, refer to the tools in this book to motivate yourself to do *something*, however small, to put you a step closer to your goal.

Mostly Bs:

The I-Have-So-Much-to-Do-I-Am-Going-to-Bed Freaker Outer

We've all been there, in that state of total overwhelm when a task looks so huge, getting it done seems impossible. This is just when you need the adrenaline to kick in most—and, yet, all at once, you run out of gas. You don't know where to start, feel completely drained, and have a sudden urge to nap.

To trick the side of you that gets spooked under pressure, learn through this book how to break up a scary-looking task into smaller, easier actions. Simply by focusing on these smaller bits one at a time, you will transform even the most intimidating task (say, a 10-page term paper on the US government) from an evil monster into a fluffy hamster in no time.

Mostly Cs:
The My-Life-Is-So-Full-It-Overfloweth (and-Drowneth-Me) Overloader

There's a little part of you that always wants more: more activities, more friends, more seashell collections, and more plastic toy ninjas. Problem is, there are not enough hours in the day—or space in your room—to pack it all in. This leaves you racing to five parties in one weekend or squishing 17 pairs of jeans into what was originally your sock drawer. In this equation, your attention is so spread out that you can't ever focus on the people, and things, that really matter to you.

If you've got loads of interests—but follow-through isn't your strong suit—this book will show you how to cut back on quantity and focus on the *quality* of things in your life. The next time you make plans for a Sunday, you'll amaze yourself by choosing just one barbecue—and having a blast—instead of rushing from place to place. If you're a music lover, you'll be inspired to whittle down your vintage album cover collection to the best 10 (okay, maybe 20) to hang on your wall. Streamlining your life may feel foreign at first, but once you've seen what it's like to enjoy (and finish) one thing at a time, you'll never go back.

Mostly Ds:

The Highly-Ambitious-Yet-Somehow-Still-Unproductive Dreamer

Like the world's most successful people, you always aim high and think big. In fact, you always have an enterprising new idea about what you're going to do next, whether it's to run a marathon or totally reorganize your life. That's a good thing. But there's just one piece missing: a plan.

A plan makes all the difference between fantasy and reality. That's why swearing you'll "clean up your act once and for all" isn't enough. To stay on track, you also need a clear course of action. This book gives you that plan and helps you on your way from dreamland to done deal.

3 Now What?

Get on the path to getting it together

No matter which (dis)organizational type you are, there is hope. Even if you fall into all four categories (which is quite an accomplishment), you can still get organized—and quickly. Just remember that, contrary to popular belief, getting organized isn't a one-time event. You have to keep at it all the time. That's why we designed this book to be used again and again. Fold down the pages you find the most helpful. Make notes in it. Get grape jelly on it. Just keep it handy so that every time you start slipping into old patterns or get stuck in a new snarl, you'll be armed and ready to restore order.

Make It Personal

Whether your goal is to organize schoolwork, schedules, or space, your most effective approach will be as unique as you are. If you know you're a visual person, make little reminders for yourself on neon green sticky notes. Or if you can't stand sticky notes, banish them from your desk forever. And, of course, if you have a system that already works great in one part of your life, leave it as is. The suggestions in this book are all helpful ideas, but the only person who can determine what works best for you is you.

One good thing to know before you start is that there's no such thing as the perfect organizing system. What matters most is establishing a routine that you can stick with over time. To do this, work *with* your little habits—even ones you don't like—instead of against them. Forget the idea that you should brainwash yourself into being someone you're not. Instead, learn to accept and live with who you actually are.

It's Not Just About Neatness

If you think being organized is only about being tidy, think again. Your friend, the movie junkie, might have a neater bedroom than yours, but if he can't get to his *Godfather* DVD at a moment's notice, the setup isn't working for him. Another friend's space might not be totally immaculate, but if she can find exactly what she's looking for at any time, the girl is organized.

If you *are* on the messy side, don't get down on yourself. It's your system that's not working—not you. The idea, here, is to find a new system. The fact that you always drop your jacket right where you are when you walk in the door doesn't make you a hopeless slob. It just means you need a hook near the door and not across the room. If your pens always end up on the desk instead of in their designated drawer, keep them on the desk in that funky green glass jar you found at a garage sale.

As you read on, remember: Being organized is about making your life easier, not harder. The whole point is that you spend less time looking for stuff and more time doing the things you want to do.

SCHOOL STUFF

SCHOOL STUFF

With the huge amount of books, homework, and handouts that you have for every class, keeping track of it all can feel like fighting a losing battle. Taking control over paper and projects is a must for peace of mind — and for keeping your grades up.

Some teachers will try to help you stay organized by telling you what kind of binders and notebooks to buy for school. But they usually don't tell you *how* to use them so that you can find stuff quickly, easily, and without inducing ulcers.

In this chapter, you'll learn how to get your school stuff together at home, in your backpack, and in your locker, so that you'll be armed and ready to tackle whatever's thrown your way.

1 Sending You an S.O.S.
Choose from 3 School Organizing Systems

We don't need to tell you how frustrating it is to lose your homework all the time—or how annoying it is when nobody believes you actually did it. It's enough to send a perfectly good student perfectly mad.

If you can relate, you need an **S.O.S.**—a School Organizing System. This is the best way to keep your schoolwork straight. For your S.O.S., you have three options: the Three-Ring Binder, the Accordion File, and the Spiral Notebook.

After checking them out, pick the one you like best. You can use the same S.O.S. for all of your subjects, or mix it up, depending on what you think will be the best for each class. Once you've chosen your system, you'll get the details on what goes in each one in the next section, **The Right Sort**.

Option #1: The Three-Ring Binder

This system uses color-tabbed dividers to determine where everything goes, and a three-hole punch to make all of your handouts binder friendly. Depending on the size of your binders and the amount of space that you need for each class, you can either give each class its own binder or use fewer binders by putting multiple subjects together. This is the most flexible S.O.S. because it lets you have as many sections as you need.

Ideal for: Classes that have tons of paper, like a current events class in which you read lots of photocopied news articles or a biology class that uses lots of handouts in addition to a textbook.

Option #2: The Accordion File

An accordion file is a stretchable folder that's divided into tabbed sections. Like the binder system on the previous page, this setup sorts papers by type. Depending on the accordion file size and the amount of space you need, each class can get its own file, or multiple classes can share one.

Ideal for: Classes that use books as their main source of materials—like a French class where you're mostly studying the textbook and don't get too many handouts.

Option #3: The Spiral Notebook System

This system centers on using notebooks for selected classes. In a spiral notebook, you keep everything from class notes to homework assignments arranged in chronological (date) order. This is a good setup if a teacher prefers spiral notebooks to binders, or if you tend to remember things by date (like that you read *The Good Earth* in June and *The Great Gatsby* in May) instead of by type (homework, class work, tests, etc.) Spiral notebooks are also less bulky than either binders or accordion files, and some people find them more comfortable to write in. Notebook paper also won't fall out as easily as binder paper, so you're less likely to have floaters roaming around your backpack.

Ideal for: Classes where the teacher asks for an interactive notebook, or any class that's relatively light on handouts but heavy on note-taking.

Option #1: The Three-Ring Binder

How it works: Every time you get a new assignment—or get back an old one—you simply put holes in it with a three-hole punch (unless it already has holes in it) and plug it into the right section. Use your color-tabbed dividers to sort papers into the following five sections for each class. (**The Right Sort**, on page 30, will explain what each section is for.)

TAB #1 TO DO	**TAB #2** CURRENT TOPIC	**TAB #3** PAST TOPICS
TAB #4 REFERENCE	**TAB #5** PAPER (keep fully stocked)	

In addition to these five, feel free to make other custom-made tabs tailored for each class, like a "vocab" section for English or a "lab" section for biology.

Essential tool: the three-hole punch
Every time you get a piece of paper that isn't prepunched, use this to get it binder ready.

When you finish an assignment at night, place it in the front of your binder. This way you always know where your homework is.

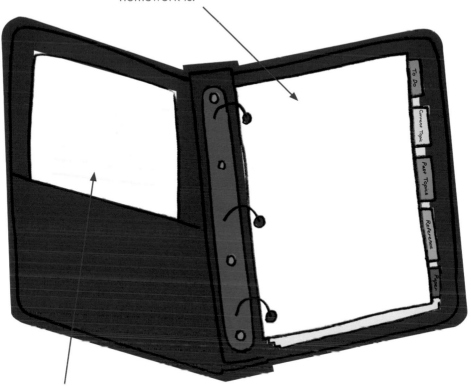

Class handouts not already punched go in the front pocket. When you get home to your three-hole punch, move them into the proper tab in your binder.

Beware: The front pocket of your binder will get full fast. To keep your system uncluttered, take a few minutes when you get home each day to punch those random papers and file them away under the proper tab.

Option #2: The Accordion File

How it works: Accordion files are great because they keep everything sorted and don't require a three-hole punch. Depending on how many you use and how full they are, they can be less bulky and fit in a backpack more easily than three-ring binders. Using accordion files also eliminates the need for additional pocket folders. It's best to use a flap-top accordion file that closes securely with Velcro or an elastic band.

For each class, papers are sorted into the following five sections, and each one gets a tab in your accordion file. (**The Right Sort**, on page 30, will explain what each section is for.)

To Do

TAB #1
TO DO

Current Topic

TAB #2
CURRENT TOPIC

Past Topics

TAB #3
PAST TOPICS

Reference

TAB #4
REFERENCE

Paper

TAB #5
PAPER
(keep fully stocked)

In addition to these five, feel free to make other custom-made tabs for each class, like a "vocab" section for English or a "lab" section for biology.

Anytime you get a handout or work returned to you in class, immediately put it in its place so that everything stays sorted.

When you finish an assignment at night, place it in the Current Topic slot. This way you always know where your homework is.

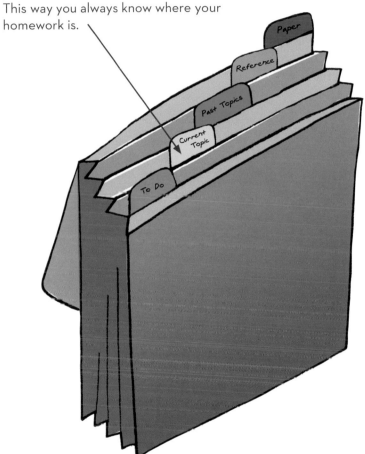

Paper

Reference

Past Topics

Current Topic

To Do

Beware: Unlike binders and notebooks, accordion files stow papers out of sight, which makes it easy to forget what's in there. To avoid overstuffed files and to keep this system running smoothly, take a few minutes each month to clear out anything you don't need and to reorganize the stuff that you do.

Option #3: The Spiral Notebook

How it works: Use separate spiral notebooks for each class. In a spiral notebook everything is automatically kept in chronological order, so make sure you actually put dates on all of your work because that's how you'll keep track of it.

Loose one-sided papers—like class calendars and handouts—get pasted, taped, or stapled directly into the notebook as soon as you get them.

Anything that can't or shouldn't be attached to a sheet of paper in the spiral notebook—including double-sided or multi-paged handouts, returned tests, or assignments to hand in—goes into a folder, color-coded to match the spiral from the same class.

Essential tool: the glue stick or stapler
Keep it with you so you're always ready to attach handouts and other papers to the pages of your notebook.

SPIRAL!

NOTE BOOK

Since you might not always have time to paste or staple handouts into your notebook while you're sitting in class, place them in your folder until you can glue or staple them in at home.

If you're using a two-pocket folder, put current handouts in the left-side pocket (1) and past ones on the right (2).

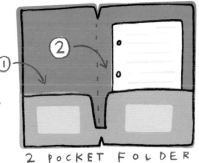

2 POCKET FOLDER

Beware: Careful gluing or stapling is key to keeping the pages from sticking together or getting too bulky. If you're at all on the sloppy side, this may not be the best system for you. Keeping everything in spiral notebooks requires daily maintenance; make sure you do regular upkeep if you choose this method.

2 | The Right Sort
Figure out what goes where

If you chose the Three-Ring Binder or Accordion File for any of your subjects, you had to make four sections for each class (plus one for blank paper); now **The Right Sort** will show you what to put in those sections. It'll also show you how to use a file box, which is handy even if you chose the Spiral Notebook for all of your classes. (Tear out The Right Sort pullout from the back of the book, and keep it with you so you're always equipped to put stuff in the right place.)

From term papers to pop quizzes, all of your papers will fall into one of the below four categories.

TAB #1: To Do

What
Anything you have not done yet (that's why it's "to do"!), including papers that relate to assignments, worksheets, or readings, you'll do outside of class. This includes whatever's in your homework planner (see planner on page 62).

Why
Instead of having to comb through your notebook to find tonight's various assignments, you can just flip straight to this section.

> # TAB #1
> # TO DO
>
> To Do
>
> ---
>
> - homework assignments
> - homework calendars
> - readings or worksheets you start in class but need to finish later
> - directions for projects or papers to be done
> - test study sheets

How
Put all stuff here until it is done. Then, once you finish any assignment, either hand it in or move it to **Current Topic.**

TAB #2: Current Topic

What

Any materials related to the topic you're currently studying in class. In history, this could be the Civil War. In biology, it could be the frog's digestive system. (File just the materials, not the frog.)

Why

When it comes time to study for a test or put together a paper or project, all your materials will be in one section.

How

Papers in this section should be stored in date order (date all of your notes and handouts). When you move onto the next topic in class, move the old papers from the **Current Topic** section into **Past Topics**.

TAB #2
CURRENT TOPIC

Current Topic

- class notes

- notes on reading you've done outside of class

- articles or printouts related to topic

- completed worksheets

- graded homework assignments

TAB #3: Past Topics

What

Any papers relating to the previous topics you've covered in class (notes about the worm that you studied before the frog, for instance). These can be worksheets, reading materials, or anything else that you're no longer covering in class. Usually, you've already been tested on this stuff.

Why

You might need these papers later for a final exam or a portfolio project, but, in the meantime, you want them out of the way so you can get to the materials you need *now* more quickly. When **Past Topics** gets full, you can move this stuff on to your file box (see page 34).

How

When you move onto a new section in class, all the materials from **Current Topic** get moved here. As they come in, put them at the back of the section so that all of your papers are still organized by date.

TAB #3
PAST TOPICS

- everything from Current Topic, once that topic is completed

- returned tests, papers, and quizzes from old topics

Past Topics

TAB #4: Reference

What

Any one-shot-deal papers that you'll need for reference throughout the semester.

Why

Because the teacher said, "Don't lose this—you're only getting it once."

How

The order of these materials doesn't matter much, since there are usually not too many class reference materials. As long as they're handy, you'll be in good shape.

TAB #4
REFERENCE

- course syllabus

- participation rubric

- information sheets
  (such as "how-to" sheets)

- reading lists

- reference sheets
  (such as the periodic table)

Your File Box

A file box is like your own miniature filing cabinet. Plastic, wooden, or metal, it sits on or near your desk and keeps files at your fingertips. Use it in these two ways.

1. Once the **Past Topics** section of your **S.O.S.** gets full or outdated, you'll need to move that stuff into a new place. This is where the file box comes in. Make a file for each class, and put the overflow here.

2. The file box is also the perfect place to put other random papers and flat stuff that you don't have a home for, whether it's future school applications, letters of recommendation from teachers, or your driver's ed certificate. You can even file that ribbon you won for best origami butterfly here. (What, you don't want to frame it?)

To keep your system streamlined, go through the file box once a month to get rid of anything you don't need anymore.

BE PREPARED

Organization lets you get things done the way you need to — but to do that, you need the right tools. Here's a list of things that every student should have at his or her disposal:

- a planner (there's one included in this book)
- pencils and pens (preferably in a pencil bag of some sort)
- sticky notes or mini writing pad
- highlighters
- a calculator
- a mini stapler
- transparent tape
- USB memory stick

The "It" List: 4 Secrets of Success

Try these little tricks to keep your new system running smoothly.

1. Color-Code It

Maybe you don't really like calculus, but maybe you love fire-engine red. Here's your chance to get organized *and* bring some style to your least-favorite subject. Color-coding means you assign one color to each class. For example, make everything (binder, folders, files) for history green, everything for English blue, and so on. When everything is color-coded, it's easy to grab exactly what you need, which means you'll never again show up to Spanish class with just your geometry notebook.

2. Date It

Write the date on all handouts, homework assignments, returned tests, and any other coursework in the top right-hand corner. This helps keep papers in order and makes it easier to see if something's missing.

3. Stick to It

No matter which of our systems you pick, the key to keeping all of them going is to file away each item as soon as you get it in your hands. This way you can skirt the law of nature that says all important papers must end up lost, trampled, or bubble-gummed together.

4. Clean It

Make an unbreakable half-hour date with yourself once a month to go through your stuff and get rid of whatever you don't need. Left to pile up, extra clutter adds unnecessary weight to your backpack and only gets in the way. This monthly sweep is also a good time to sort any loose papers that need to find a home (returned trig homework, notes to your last crush, frame-worthy doodles) and to neaten things up in general. Put your cleanup date in your planner.

3 Your Digital Desktop
Keep computer files organized

All of this paper sorting won't do any good if your computer is still in disarray. Organizing digital files is just as important as the other stuff—especially if you do most of your homework on screen. Try this method to keep your computer in order and your digital files easy to find.

School Folder

Create a folder on your hard drive for all school-related stuff. To lighten things up, give it a fun nickname that makes it clear that it belongs to you (and not your weird cousin who always uses your computer when he visits). Then create an alias (or shortcut icon) on your desktop so you can get to your stuff fast.

Grade Folders

Make one folder for each year of school (10th grade, 11th grade) and put them in the main folder.

Class Folders

Create a separate folder for each subject you're taking (English, astronomy).

Topic Folders

Add subfolders within each Class Folder for whatever it needs, like "World War I" for History, or "Macbeth" for English.

SAVE AS

If you're working on a second draft of a paper or project, don't save over the original. Instead, do a "Save As" and name the versions "Macbeth_essay_1," "Macbeth_essay_2," and so on. This is smart for two reasons: First, if something happens to the new file, you still have the older draft to work from instead of having to starting over. Second, it gives you the option of reverting to the original version if you decide you liked it better before.

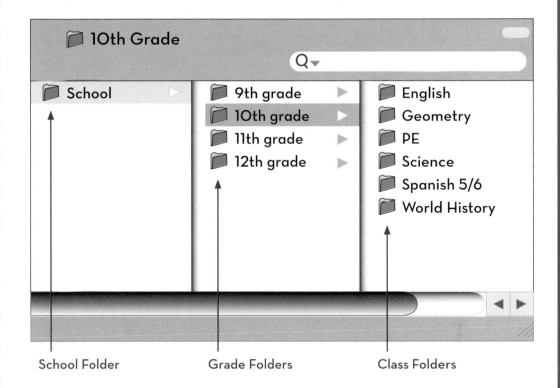

School Folder   Grade Folders   Class Folders

Back It Up and Bring It Along

You probably know by now that having a good system for transporting digital files from one place to the next is a total necessity. If you start a project on another computer at school, the library, or a friend's house, you need a quick, reliable way to get your document home, or vice versa.

Backing stuff up is also super important. If you're like most people, your life is on your computer. That makes losing your hard drive due to theft or system error a very scary thought. Protect your files (and your sanity) by backing up all of your important docs at least once a week. This way, if you lose something on your computer, all the brilliant work you've done won't just go poof.

The charts on the next pages show different ways to both transfer and back up your files. Use at least two methods at all times so that even if one fails, you can still save a trip to the asylum.

Here's How to Transfer and Back Up Files

METHOD	DESCRIPTION	GOOD FOR BACKING UP FILES	GOOD FOR BRINGING ALONG
email	Send the document to yourself as an attachment. (We always like this trick because it's fast, reliable, and free.) WH••SH!		✔
USB	Use a USB memory stick, which lets you save files in one place and then transfer them to your own hard drive later. Just make sure the memory stick is compatible with both machines. Memory sticks are affordable and easy to use, but they're also small and can get lost easily. If you're using one, put your name on it and keep it in an inside pocket of your backpack where it will be safe from damage, loss, or sticky fingers (yours and other people's).	✔	✔

METHOD	DESCRIPTION	GOOD FOR BACKING UP FILES	GOOD FOR BRINGING ALONG
free online storage	Sign up with an online server like savefile.com or box.net, which will let you drag and drop files to store on the Web for free.	✔	✔
iPod	Attach an iPod or other MP3 player to your computer, then drag and drop files onto it.		✔
external hard drive	Use this handy little gizmo to save everything on your computer's internal hard drive.	✔	
CD	CDs are great for archiving everything from a particular semester or class once it's over, though relying on them for everyday saving and transporting could get expensive and wasteful, since you can use them only once each. When using CDs, burn a disc and label it clearly with whatever's on it. Keep your CDs labeled (with dates on them) and neatly organized (by those dates) in either a CD file box, shoe box, or designated drawer. Name each CD in a way that makes it easy to recognize what the contents are (example: art history, 9th grade).	✔	✔

4 Make a Home Base
Set up your perfect work space at home

As you've noticed (and often tried to forget), a lot of "schoolwork" is really work that happens at home. To get it all done—and find it again later—you need a **Home Base**, a dedicated place at home arranged to suit just you. A good Home Base has two essential parts that are usually side by side: a **Drop-Off Station** and a **Study Space**.

The Drop-Off Station

The **Drop-Off Station** is just what the name suggests: It's your total drop-off and pick-up spot for all school-related stuff. This is where you dump all your stuff when you stop off at home between football practice and your part-time job at the video store. It's also where you store books, organize papers, and load up on everything you need for the day. Ideally, it should be located right next to your **Study Space**, so that all of your stuff stays together.

WEIRD AUNT GAVE YOU THIS

THE WORLD AT YOUR FINGER-TIPS!

BINDERS & TEXTBOOKS

EXTRA PAPER & THREE-HOLE PUNCH

BINS WITH EXTRA SCHOOL SUPPLIES

FILE BOX

BACKPACK

The Study Space

Your **Study Space** is where you're free to create, brainstorm, and ponder life's questions. It's also where you do homework. The point of a Study Space is to make studying less painful (enjoyable, even) by making your surroundings as welcoming as possible. Your Study Space has a desk and is also the main hub for all your school stuff—printer, paper, file box, and supplies.

Study Space Necessities

Good lighting

It's hard to work if you can't see what you are working on. The best study setups include two light sources: an overhead lamp that lights the room overall, plus a smaller desk lamp that puts more focused light where you need it.

Comfort

If the chair is too high or you have to strain your neck and shoulders to see the computer, you'll be itching to get away instead of feeling inspired to start that enthralling essay on ant behavior.

Elbow room

Make sure there's enough space to spread out piles of books *and* to work on your computer at the same time.

Print Protocol

In a perfect world, everyone would have a printer in their own room. (And the printers would do our homework for us.) But alas, it's not a perfect world, and some of us have to share. So, if you don't have a printer in your **Study Space**, make sure the family printer is easily accessible.

If you don't have a home printer at all or find that yours is not always reliable (or always running low on ink), know the locations of other printers that work with your computer. These can be anywhere nearby, like a friend's house, the library, a parent's office, or your friendly neighborhood copy store. Choose one as your official Plan B—that way you'll have a go-to place already lined up if your own printer poops out.

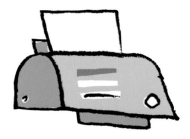

Study Outside the Box

Although we recommend using your **Study Space** for homework most of the time, there are some times when the work you're doing is better suited to another spot. For example, a comfy window seat is the perfect place to curl up and read. Alternative workspaces can be anything from the family room to the backyard, the kitchen table to your dad's old desk in the attic. No little nook is too weird, as long as it suits your task and gets your brain waves moving. And if sprawling on the floor is more your speed, feel free. Just don't make your work space so comfy that you wake up drooling on your homework three hours after you started it. If you work a lot in any high-traffic family zone, designate one fixed spot in that room where you can put your school stuff when you need to get it out of the way quickly (a shelf, a box, the bread drawer). Having this go-to storage spot makes it easy to find your stuff again later—and keeps it safe from sibling wreckage and spaghetti-sauce splatter.

Make It You

Your **Home Base** needs to be useful, but it should also be inspiring. No matter how perfect the setup is on paper, the fact is you won't like sitting at a desk that's all cluttered. Keep the space neat and inviting with things you love to look at, like bright decorative folders, a funky lamp, or a personally designed box that holds your art supplies. Save some space on your tack board for pics of best friends, an autographed baseball ticket, or whatever reflects your current passions and drives you to kick some butt.

W.O.W
words of wisdom

RECYCLE AND REPURPOSE

For a work space that's environmentally friendly, cheap to create, *and* completely unique, try these creative ideas:

- Turn a tired tool or tackle box into an organizing tray for school supplies like scissors, stapler, sticky notes, and index cards.
- Line up large seashells to hold paper clips, binder clips, and rubber bands.
- Use a plastic egg crate for hanging files.
- Transform a river rock into an all-natural paperweight.

5 Backpack Basics
Get the scoop on selecting schoolbags

An everyday style statement, the right backpack has a special place in your heart—and on your back. That means it should look good on the shelf, feel good when you're wearing it, and do what it's supposed to do (which is carry your life around for you). The first step to finding the right pack is to make a list of everything you need for school, sports, part-time jobs, and your other activities, so you can see just how big it needs to be. On top of all your everyday textbooks and school supplies, here are some of the things your list might include:

- gym clothes (don't worry—they take up the same space dirty or clean)
- clothing, gear, or instruments for hockey practice, dance class, trumpet lessons, or any other extracurricular pursuits
- books for after-school tutoring
- work clothes (if you have an after-school job)
- lunch (unless you buy it at school)
- water bottle
- snacks, gum, mints, and such
- personal stuff like deodorant (for post-gym), Band-Aids (for blisters and paper cuts), and allergy medicine (for that uncontrollable spring sneezing)

OK, now start your own:
- _____
- _____
- _____
- _____
- _____
- _____

Pick a Schoolbag That Works

Size it up

Once you have a complete list, gather all of the stuff that's on it and throw it into a big old heap on the floor. Doing this will give you a good idea of what size bag you'll need. Plus, it's an excuse to make a mess.

Sort it out

Choose a bag with multiple compartments, pockets, or dividers so you can separate your stuff by type, like books and binders in the big section, and smaller stuff like a calculator, pencil bag, and snacks in the smaller sections.

Secure it inside

An inside zip pocket is useful for keeping important stuff (the kind that your parents would kill you if you lost) like keys, money, and your ID.

Double Bag It

Two bags?! Isn't one schoolbag more than enough? Well, that depends on the quantity of stuff you have to carry and how often you need it. A second bag is a great idea to keep after-school stuff separate. This way your main bag will be lighter, and you can put the second bag in your locker or another safe place once you get to school. The only potential downside is that your stuff is now divided up rather than consolidated in one place. So, just make sure things like art supplies don't get accidentally divided between your two bags. Your sketch pad will be lonely (and your art teacher unsympathetic) if you show up to art class without your drawing pencils.

If you do decide to use a second bag in addition to your main one, choose the shape based on the stuff you're putting in it. For example, a duffel bag is good for holding sports stuff, and a messenger bag is good for art supplies.

Keep Your Back Happy

Back padding

This keeps your back protected from pointy objects like renegade binder corners and bulky textbooks.

Two adjustable straps

These help distribute the weight evenly across your shoulders so you'll be upright and able-bodied for rugby practice in the spring.

Lightweight materials

Don't be macho. The lighter the bag, the less weight you'll have to carry around, and tough guy or no, you'll be thankful.

Waist strap

Agreed, it's not exactly a fashion statement but it's better than a back brace. If your bag gets so heavy your back starts to hurt, a waist strap can shift some of the weight to your hips. (Backpackers use these all the time.)

To Roll or Not to Roll?

Backpacks with wheels can be great if you've been injured or if you're in too many honors classes and have 16-plus textbooks. There are even some cool-looking ones that won't make you feel like an old lady on the way to buy groceries. But the wheels themselves, and the extra structure they require, can add weight to the bag, which means it's heavier to haul when you do need to carry it. If you do decide to use one, make sure that the handle is long enough so that you don't have to stoop to use it.

PICK-UP TIPS

Most back injuries happen during liftoff, so resist the urge to grab your bag and sling it over your shoulder like it's your little sister. Instead, bend your knees and lift it using the strength of your legs. Put on one shoulder strap at a time and go.

6 Befriend Your Backpack
Tame that beast once and for all

When used the right way, a backpack is an ergo-friendly, efficient way to haul stuff around. Used the wrong way, it's a gigantic, scary hump brimming with mangled old photocopies, an army of chocolate bar wrappers, and every textbook you have ever owned.

Besides creating serious stress on your back, an overstuffed bag is a beast that's notorious for gobbling up important papers. If you're going to work at top capacity during the day, your backpack needs to be like an organized friend who keeps everything you need nearby and neat. This means that not everything has to be in your bag at all times. Check out this easy daily routine, guaranteed to tame the beast once and for all.

The Daily Drop

Get in the habit of emptying your backpack every day when you get home from school at your **Drop-Off Station**. Use these four steps.

Step #1: Unload

Dump everything out onto the floor or a table. Feel free to make a mess—for a moment.

Step #2: Sort

Stack textbooks, notebooks, and binders onto their designated shelves. Toss out any trash that you've collected throughout the day, including crumpled bits of paper, lint-covered mints, and that tag you ripped off your sweater and then stuffed, for some reason, in your math book.

Step #3: File, Punch, or Glue

Pull out any loose papers, like handouts or graded tests, that you may have just stuck in randomly during the day. Move these to the right places in your binder, folder, or notebook.

Step #4: Toss

Do a weekly cleanup to keep your backpack lean and mean. Fridays are perfect for this—this way you get to start the next week with less stuff bouncing around behind you. Toss any trash, and sort everything else into your **S.O.S.** (see page 22).

Preparation Makes Perfect

Nothing messes with your sanity like starting off the day with a frantic search for last night's homework between bites of toast, butter dripping steadily onto your shirt. You can eliminate this panicked portion of your morning by simply packing up everything you need the night before. Before you go to bed each night quickly run through your class schedule and planner, gather your books and assignments, and get ready to roll. The next day you might actually have time for breakfast—on a real plate.

Backpack Checklist

Use this checklist to get packed in seconds flat. (See the back of this book for a pullout version, which you can personalize, add to, and post somewhere at your **Home Base**.)

THE GOODS	PACKED?
textbooks for each class	
binders, notebooks, or files for each class, including whatever assignments are due	
planner	
pens and pencils	
calculator	
gym clothes	
after-school activity equipment and sports gear	
wallet	
ID/bus pass	
keys	
cell phone	
water bottle	
USB memory stick	

7 Doctor Your Locker
Love your metal-box-away-from-home

Not everyone has a locker, but if you do, you should make the most of it. Contrary to popular belief, a locker can be more than just a purgatory for petrified gym shoes. Instead, think of it as a smaller, off-site version of your **Home Base**. This is the place that grounds you throughout the day and keeps you feeling free instead of weighted down like a pack mule. So say good-bye to the fear of what you'll find behind that squeaky steel door.

Your Own Personal Gallery

You've got your own style. You've also got three different crushes, opinions on school politics, a passion for sunflowers, and an inexplicable obsession with reptiles. Express yourself every time you open your locker by covering the inside door with things that tell people who you are.

Use these ideas for inspiration:

- vintage magnets
- snapshots of friends and family
- CD covers and magazine cutouts
- photos of your dream car
- small mounted mirror to check your look on the way to class
- mounted sticky notes or whiteboard

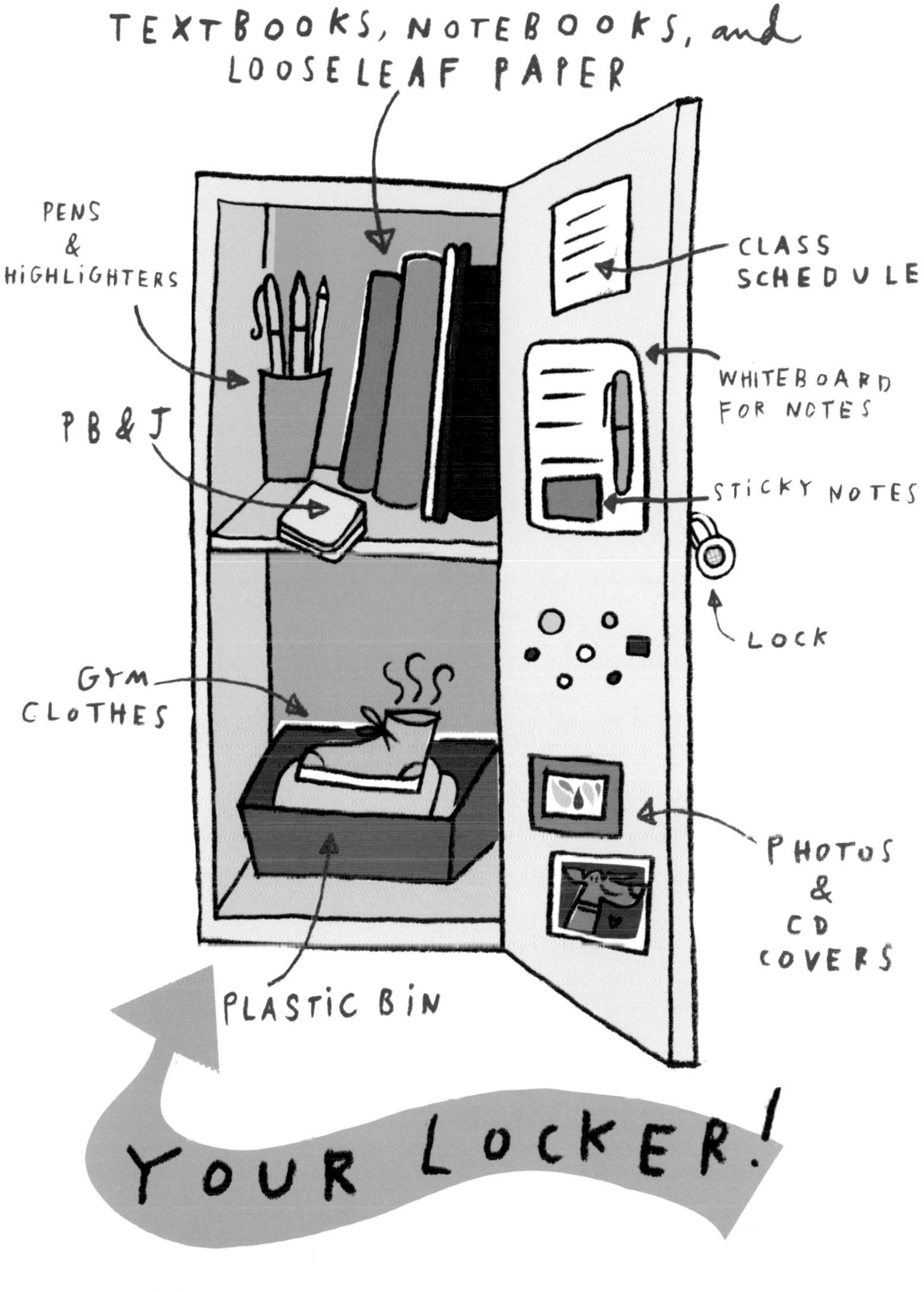

TEXTBOOKS, NOTEBOOKS, and LOOSELEAF PAPER

PENS & HIGHLIGHTERS

CLASS SCHEDULE

PB & J

WHITEBOARD FOR NOTES

STICKY NOTES

LOCK

GYM CLOTHES

PHOTOS & CD COVERS

PLASTIC BIN

YOUR LOCKER!

TIME AND ACTIVITIES

TIME AND ACTIVITIES

In this ultra-busy world, it's sometimes hard to decide where to focus your energy. Friends, homework, sports, emails, and calls to return—all of these crowd your brain and clamor for attention. It's no secret that there's never enough time to do every single thing you want to do. Learning to plan and prioritize is the only way to make sure that the things that matter the most to you—family, friends, perfecting your keyboard rendition of "Chopsticks"—get the time they deserve.

True efficiency is not rushing frantically from place to place, task to task. Instead, it's the feeling of ease that comes with a clear mind. When you have a plan for the day, you can stop stressing about what to do next. This leaves you free to just relax and enjoy the moment—even if all you're doing is feeding the dog.

In this chapter you'll learn the skills you need to put time on your side. You'll also get the blueprints for the perfect personal planner, an essential tool for making every day more efficient—and less hectic—than you ever dreamed possible.

1 The Brain Dump
Get it off your head and onto paper

Like it or not, you're a walking to-do list. Urgent tasks, not-so-urgent tasks, tasks you'd love to do if you had endless time and cash — every waking hour, these thoughts compete for space in your brain. Without a reliable way to track these to-dos, that mental storm can put you in a state of perma-panic that distracts you from the present and makes it harder to get things done.

The Brain Dump is a proven method for turning the muffled static in your head into clear-signal action. This mental exercise allows you to get everything out of your brain, so that you can put it all back in again — in an organized way. Basically, it's like rebooting your brain every time you need a fresh start.

Get It Down

Start with a blank sheet of paper and spend 10 to 15 minutes jotting down all your to-dos. Nothing's too huge or too puny for this list. (Feel free to put "apply to college" next to "buy shampoo.") See the example on the next page.

○	## SAMPLE BRAIN DUMP
	study for math test
	call Matt
	text Scott about borrowing CD
	organize closet
	go to doctor, Tues. 4:00
	buy paper, pens
	make brownies for bake sale
	meet at Kyle's house, Sat. 10 am
	write English paper
○	email Sophie back
	buy new jeans
	train for triathlon
	fold sweaters
	send thank-you note to Mom's friend (name?? ask Mom)
	put summer photos in album
	send out Halloween party invites!
	start running every day
	go to soccer game, Fri. 5:30 (bring chips for team)
	search online for power smoothie recipe
○	learn to snowboard
	redecorate room
	feed Smitty

Now try one yourself:

	MY BRAIN DUMP
◯	
◯	
◯	

Brain Dump Tips

1. Know Your Verbage

As you write each item on your list, start it with a verb. This takes a to-do from a fuzzy concept of something that has to get done to a clear course of action. Even if you already know the action, write the verb anyway. When it comes time to do each task, you'll be glad it's laid out so simply. Here are a few examples:

FUZZY (NO VERB) ⟶ CLEAR ACTION (WITH VERB)

Scott's CD ⟶ **text** Scott about borrowing CD

thank-you note/Mom's friend ⟶ **send** thank-you note to Mom's friend

sweaters ⟶ **fold** sweaters

2. Decide Not to Decide

Avoid starting a to-do with the word "decide." Nine times out of ten, a decision to be made is actually just an action waiting to be defined. For example, if you need to figure out which snowboard to buy, your action could be, "Read up on snowboards online." If you have to decide what to wear to a party, your action might be, "Rip apart closet and frantically try on every item I own, then go borrow the same sweater I always borrow from Alisa." You get the picture.

Break It Down

Now that you have your list, sort everything in it into one of the following three categories. Have a notebook nearby that's reserved especially for **Brain Dump** sorting.

1. Do Now

Apply the three-minute rule: If you can do it in three minutes or less, just get it out of the way now. You can't beat the satisfaction that comes with clearing these quickies from your list—especially when you cross each thing off as you go. **Do Now** things do not get entered in your notebook.

○	SAMPLE BRAIN DUMP	
	study for math test	
	NOW ~~call Matt~~	
	NOW ~~text Scott about borrowing CD~~	
	organize closet	
	go to doctor, Tues. 4:00	
	buy paper, pens	
	make brownies for bake sale	
	meet at Kyle's house, Sat. 10 am	
	write English paper	
○	**NOW** ~~email Sophie back~~	
	buy new jeans	
	train for triathlon	
	NOW ~~fold sweaters~~	
	NOW ~~send thank you note to Mom's friend (name?? ask Mom)~~	
	put summer photos in album	
	send out Halloween party invites!	
	start running every day	
	go to soccer game, Fri. 5:30 (bring chips for team)	
	search online for power smoothie recipe	
○	learn to snowboard	
	redecorate room	
	NOW ~~feed Smitty~~	

2. Do Soon

Everything in this category has three things in common. One, they take more than three minutes to do. Two, they are realistically possible to achieve in the near future (that means no note on Wednesday to "train for *this* weekend's triathlon"). Three, they are important to you or to someone you love.

DO SOON

study for math test
organize closet
buy paper, pens
make brownies for bake sale
write English paper
buy new jeans
send out Halloween party invites!
search online for power smoothie recipe

FIND JEANS

Take your notebook and jot down all **Do Soon** items onto the first page. As you take care of **Do Soon** things throughout the week, cross them off the list. Don't panic if they don't all get done. At the end of the week, just rip out that list, copy whatever's left to do onto a fresh page, then add whatever new tasks have come up. This way you can always refer to one consolidated list at the front of your notebook, instead of flipping through it to find bits and pieces of old lists.

3. Do Someday

Even if something isn't doable for you right now, it's still important to preserve the idea. This makes it more likely to happen in the future and lets you relax in the knowledge that your dreams won't be forgotten.

DO SOMEDAY

train for triathlon
put summer photos in album
start running every day
learn to snowboard
redecorate room

Using the last page of that same notebook, write down your **Do Someday** list and add to it over time as you think of new things. When you update your **Do Soon** list each week, read over your **Do Someday** list to see whether you're ready to move any items to the front. You may even find that you've achieved a few of your goals without knowing it.

Appointments

Anything on your list that's time-specific, meaning it *has* to be done on a particular day and time, goes in your planner (which you'll learn about on page 62). For now, just mark a **P** next to it.

		SAMPLE BRAIN DUMP
	○	
		study for math test
		call Matt
		text Scott about borrowing CD
		organize closet
P		go to doctor, Tues. 4:00
		buy papers, pens
		make brownies for bake sale
P		meet at Kyle's house, Sat. 10 am
		write English paper
	○	email Sophie back
		buy new jeans
		train for triathlon
		fold sweaters
		send thank-you note to Mom's friend (name?? ask Mom)
		put summer photos in album
		send out Halloween party invites!
		start running every day
P		go to soccer game, Fri. 5:30 (bring chips for team)
		search online for power smoothie recipe
	○	learn to snowboard
		re-decorate room
		feed Smitty

Why The Brain Dump Works

It works for two reasons. First, your subconscious brain can't tell the difference between realistic to-dos and goals that may not be possible, given the amount of time or money you have right now. As a result, your mind could be muddled with both the doable and the impossible—and unable to accomplish either. When you put each goal down on paper, it becomes easier to see it clearly and decide whether it's realistic. If it's not, you can either 1) adjust the goal to make it doable or 2) ditch it altogether. Neither of these things can happen when things are just floating around in your head.

Another benefit of **The Brain Dump** is that it forces you to define your goals, which is the first step to turning them into action. In fact, the act of writing down goals, even random ones that seem like wishful thinking (like "master the didgeridoo"), makes them much more likely to happen.

TRY IT ▶ PAPER IMPOSSIBLE

The Problem ▼

You have an eight-page research paper due next Friday. Every time you think of it, you feel this awful sense of dread about how hard it's going to be to write—and what will happen if you don't get it done. This thought is so nerve-wracking that you tell yourself you'll deal with it later and push it to the back of your mind, where it slowly drives you stark raving mad.

Bottom Line ▼

You're right: The thought of writing an eight-page research paper is totally intimidating—when looked at as a whole. But break up the project into a series of small steps (called an **Action List**) and the vicious gorilla shrinks down to a cute little gnome.

Project: Write an Eight-Page History Paper
Action List:
Sit down at my desk.
Read the assignment over.
Open a new file in my computer, name it, and save it.
Jot down questions that I need to research.
Search the Web and/or go to the library.
Read over notes I've compiled from the research, and highlight the info I need for my paper.
Make a general outline of the paper.
Write one paragraph.
Write some more.
Read it over once.
Correct any typos I find and add anything else I missed.
Read it over again.
Be done!

What To Do ▼

Think of a task you've been putting off because it's just too hideous to look at, then list the steps needed to complete it. The Action List can be as long you want and as literal as "pick up my pen from the desk." When you're through, try doing the steps one by one, without worrying about the big picture. Before you know it, you'll be done.

2 Dealing With Deadlines
Create your own personalized planner

It's time to create a personal planner, that all-important key to taking control of your time. You might think that planners are just for stuffy executives wearing bad suits and even worse shoes. But it's not true. Planners are for anyone who wants to have a plan—and that includes you.

Now, this is the fun part: You get to make your own planner. The planner template in the back of this book was created for teens, to suit your schedule and your life. To create your own personalized school planner, take the pull-out template in the back of the book and photocopy it for each week of school, then bind it together.

Making your planner

1. Count
Check how many weeks are in your school year.

2. Copy
Photocopy the pull-out planner in the back of the book at 130%, then make enough copies for each week in your school year.

3. Bind
Three-hole punch your planner and put it into a three-ring binder, or have it bound by your local copy store.

How to use your planner

In order for you to get the benefits that come with using a planner, make one that's complete and reliable. Follow these planner "dos" and "don'ts" to ensure you are getting the most out of using your planner.

Do

- write your name and phone number on the first page of your planner
- take out your planner at the beginning of each class and put it on your desk
- put everything in the same planner, whether it's math homework or a soccer game
- consult your planner when you get home to see what you need to do that night

Don't

- forget your planner at home
- jot down appointments on the backs of birthday cards or torn up bits of cafeteria napkin
- use a second planner that's "just for school" or "just for social stuff"

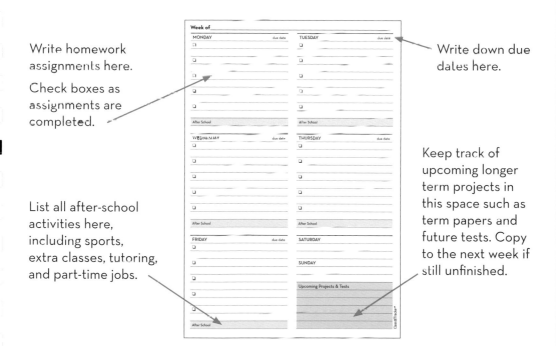

Write homework assignments here.

Check boxes as assignments are completed.

List all after-school activities here, including sports, extra classes, tutoring, and part-time jobs.

Write down due dates here.

Keep track of upcoming longer term projects in this space such as term papers and future tests. Copy to the next week if still unfinished.

3 Time Check
See where your hours are really going

One common time-budgeting blunder people make is confusing the amount of time things *should* take with the amount of time they actually do take. This brand of wishful thinking leads to all kinds of real-life messes, from chronic lateness and broken promises to constant feelings of being scattered and overwhelmed.

Take a look at what a little half-baked time budgeting does to the average morning routine:

ROUTINE TASK	BUDGETED TIME	ACTUAL TIME
Snooze button hits	1 (5 minutes)	3 (15 minutes)
Shower	5 minutes	10 minutes
Get dressed	5 minutes	15 minutes
Breakfast	10 minutes	20 minutes
Pack lunch	10 minutes	5 minutes
Total Time	35 minutes	65 minutes

Total Lateness = 30 minutes

And that's just before 8 am.

To budget your time accurately, you need to know how long things really take. Over the next week, make a point of timing different everyday tasks: doing your math homework, calling a friend, or putting on your elephant costume for drama rehearsal. Depending on your personality and the way you do things, the actual time it takes to do something can be anywhere from half as long to three times as long as you esti-mate. Jot down the real time that each task takes so you can check back on it later as you're planning your schedule.

Once you get a sense of how long things really take compared with what you're used to thinking they do, you'll get better at hitting the mark. When in doubt, always err on the side of over-budgeting time rather than risking getting caught short.

Trust the Clock

Resist the urge to ignore the results of your timing experiment, and avoid the tempt-ing resolution to keep it shorter "next time." It's all too easy to make excuses for why getting dressed took longer *today*. After all, you never could have predicted that the sweater you were planning to wear had a new hole in it — one that suspiciously matched the points on your brother's new ski poles. Problem is, every day is full of those annoying little surprises that tack on extra time (a late bus, a missing sock, or your older sister "borrowing" your hair dryer again). Plan for the unexpected. The worst thing that can happen is that you'll have a few extra minutes to relax between tasks. Imagine that.

4 Activity Overload
Step down from the merry-go-round

Even with great organizing skills and the perfect planner, there's only so much stuff a person can cram into one day. Sports practice, dance lessons, debate clubs, part-time jobs, and other after-school activities — it's tempting to try to pack it all in.

While it's good to challenge yourself and keep learning different things, it's easy to cross the line from healthy activity to perpetual frenzy. A too-packed schedule can leave you buckling under pressure, big time. And it can also make you sick. Head-aches, stomachaches, or constant worry and exhaustion come directly from overex-tending yourself. And there are other signs that you might be doing too much: missing deadlines, being late a lot, and breaking promises (you keep *meaning* to watch your best friend's skateboard practice, but you never actually get there).

When life is busy, one way to avoid burnout is to make a little time to be perfectly unproductive every single day—away from the TV, phone, and computer. How to do that? Rub the dog's belly. Dance around your room to a song you'd never be caught dead listening to in public. Make the world's longest rubber-band chain. Taking time to do something trivial on a daily basis helps you slow down, lighten up, and keep your silly side intact. Can't find the time? That's why you have to *make* it. Otherwise there will always be something else that seems more important, and the goal here is to take a break from the important stuff (it will still be there later).

5 The Deciding Factor

Make decisions — and stick with them

Oddly enough, many people waste a big chunk of time just trying to decide how to spend it. Indecision about what to do next also multiplies stress by making everything take longer. Let's face it, if you're agonizing over what to do tonight, you're probably not totally focused on the book you're reading right now. Which means that now you have to go back and read this paragraph again. And then maybe again.

If good time budgeting lets you glide through life with ease, indecision is the trap that can keep you in tangles. The good news: You have practically endless choices for how to spend your time. The bad news: You have practically endless choices for how to spend your time. What to focus on, who to spend time with, what activities to do, which one to do *first* … you're faced with so many choices every day, it's no mystery why decision-making skills are so important in getting the most from your time.

But for some people, making decisions has all the appeal of scraping taffy off a shoe. Why is that? Most decision-phobes are usually stuck on the myth that by making a choice, they're limiting their options. In fact, the reverse is true: Most opportunities have deadlines, and by letting the clock run out on them without making a decision, options get eliminated and decisions get made for you … whether they're the right ones or not.

The next time indecision sets your inner compass spinning, try these simple techniques to figure out what you *really* want to do.

Dilemma Remedy #1: The Weigh Station

To break through doubt about what to do, make a **Weigh Station** on paper so that all the benefits and drawbacks of each option are laid out for you to see. Once you get it all down on paper, the answer will likely pop up. This technique is great for comparing anywhere from 2 choices to 10. To see how the Weigh Station works, take a look at this example.

DILEMMA: Should I go to Greg's lacrosse game OR see Lisa's play on Saturday night?

Go to Greg's lacrosse game	See Lisa's play
Said I would go	Oops ... said I would go
His games are fun	I haven't seen a play in a while
Greg's my best friend	I flaked on Lisa's last play
There are only 3 games left this year	Saturday is the only night I can see it

DEAL BREAKER

VERDICT: GO SEE LISA'S PLAY

Dilemma Remedy #2: Talk It Out

If you're stuck in indecision, sometimes it helps to run through the dilemma with a friend or family member you trust. The idea here isn't to ask them what you should do; it's to get clear on what you want to do by talking through it aloud. Because you're more interested in what your own heart is saying than in the opinions of others, bypass the well-meaning friend who always "knows" the answers, and pick someone who's just a really good listener. (And avoid making the rounds—one person is plenty.)

PICK AND STICK

When you've made a decision, stick with it. The only reason to change your mind after that is if you get new facts that change the picture completely. Otherwise, trust your own judgment and stay true to your choice.

Dilemma Remedy #3: The Coin Flip

Sometimes you can struggle with a decision for days, while deep down you've already made up your mind. To trick your brain into spilling its secret, flip a coin to make your decision. Chances are you'll find yourself rooting for one side over the other as you flip. Or, you may feel a pang of disappointment with the way the coin falls. If so, you'll know you really wanted the other option all along. Mind-bluffing mission accomplished.

THE DE-FREEZE

All the worrying over making a mistake spooks some people into a frozen state of fear in which they can't do anything at all. When faced with this kind of indecision, sometimes the only cure is just a good old-fashioned kick in the butt.

If fear of making the wrong move is keeping you from moving at all, just make a choice — any choice — and then get on with it. Decision-making is a learned skill, which means that it gets easier every time you do it. The worst thing that can happen is that you'll make a mistake and learn from it. That's still a million times better than doing nothing and missing out.

YOUR ROOM

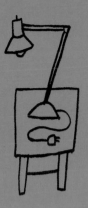

YOUR ROOM

With the amount of time you spend in it, your room should be the most welcoming, rewarding, and inspiring place you can possibly be. But being "at home" is about much more than surrounding yourself with familiar stuff. The true meaning of home is having the comfort and convenience of doing things easily—and the way you want. What does this have to do with being organized? Everything. It's this state of comfort, not so-called tidiness, that's the true sign of an organized life.

The first rule of organizing a room is also the first rule of interior design: Arrange your space based on the way you really use it. That's why architects everywhere always begin projects by interviewing their clients about how they live and what inspires them most. This way, the architect can design a space that not only matches a client's lifestyle, but also points to the activities the client wants to do more of. For the lead singer in a band, the architect might add a mini recording studio. For a movie buff, a home theater.

The second rule of organizing a room is to make the most of the space you have. That includes not only putting things In places that make sense to your lifestyle, but also clearing out stuff that you no longer need. This can be a challenge, but there are some tricks that make it easy—and even fun.

In this chapter, you'll learn how to maximize your space and arrange your room to reflect the way you want to live in it.

Space Out
Find the room inside your room

One trick shared by both professional organizers and interior designers is to create multiple "rooms" within a room—different sections devoted to different activities. We call these **Spaces**. Breaking your room into Spaces looks cool, makes everyday tasks more efficient, and keeps everything you need at your fingertips. It also just plain gives you more "space."

Even if you share a room, you can still get the benefits of breaking it up into smaller sections. In fact, this method helps keep the peace by allowing room-sharers to do different activities without getting in each other's hair.

Your Spaces should reflect the way you live—and the way you want to live. Every bedroom has basic Spaces like **Study Spaces** and **Sleep Spaces**, but you can also create ones tailor-made for you, like a **Dance Space**, **Music Space**, or **Yoga Space**.

Map It Out

Now it's time for *you* to become the interior designer. Think of your room as a blank slate. How would *you* like to live in it?

Referring to the map on the right as an example, grab a sheet of paper and sketch out how you'd like your room to look. Start with the basic Spaces you know you'll need for the things you already do. Next, write down any other Spaces you'd like to create for the things you'd *like* to do, such as a **Painting Space** with art supplies and an easel, a **Music Space** where you keep your CD player, iPod, and music, or a **Workout Space** that contains your free weights or enough floor space to do Pilates. Add these sections to your map even if you think they won't fit. You may not have the room now, but as you go through this chapter and clean out and rearrange your stuff, that may change.

You'll come back to this map later, after you've cleared things out a bit and are ready to start moving stuff around.

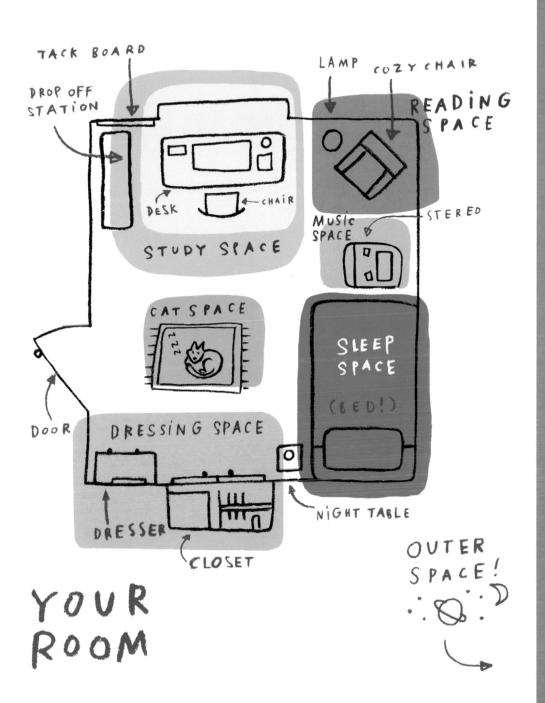

YOUR
ROOM

Finding Space(s) in a Small Room

Small rooms have it rough. They get blamed for messes, accused of losing things, and generally scorned. But don't slander your stomping grounds — even if your room makes a shoe box look luxurious, it's what you do with it that counts.

As you saw on the last page, dividing a room into **Spaces** by activity lets you make the most of every inch. And when you're living on a small scale, that's more important than ever.

Those with mini living quarters can also maximize space by looking at their rooms on three levels, starting from the ground up.

Level #1: The Floor

If space is tight, see if you can swap out your wide dressers for taller, narrower pieces that offer the same storage, but take up less floor space. Naturally, you'll have to check in with your folks about buying new furniture. Flea markets, thrift stores, and garage sales are great places to find used furniture at bargain prices.

Level #2: Unused Surfaces

These are prime places to stack boxes, desktop organizers, and cabinets that can go on top of your existing furniture to extend storage space upward.

Level #3: The Walls

Put blank wall space to use with shelves, display cabinets, and other hangable organizing options.

Also ...

No matter what size your space, identify any bulky furniture that might be better off gone—like that old leather chair that you never sit in or that octagonal table that you're always walking into. Stuff like this is just awkward and unnecessary; swap it out for free floor space instead.

 **TRY IT ▶ MOVE IT!**

The Problem

Your closet's top shelf is overflowing with sweaters, T-shirts, and sweats Since the shelf is taller than you, you're constantly forced to jump up and grab the edge of whatever you want to wear. This inevitably makes the whole pile topple to the floor. Finally, you give up and start leaving everything in a heap at the bottom of the closet. Why bother if it's going to end up on the floor anyway, decorated with shoeprints?

Bottom Line

You need to get to those clothes every single day, which means they need to be accessible, easy to see, and easy to put back later. The tall height of the shelf makes it a better location for something you use less often, like that untouched collection of board games in the trunk by your bed. By swapping the locations of these two things, you'll make better use of your storage space—and you won't walk around with shoeprints on your back anymore.

What To Do

Take two minutes now to look at your room and your closet. Sometimes you get so used to putting something in a certain place, you don't even notice how annoying it is to keep it there. Spot something that's always getting in your way, and jot it down. Be as specific as you can, like, "I'm constantly rummaging around in that bin for the right lacrosse gear," or "My hats always fall off those tiny hooks." Now write down a few ideas about how to make it work better. The solutions will be simpler than you think.

2 Make Your Space Make Sense
Look at what's working and what's not

While most rooms have things that need to be fixed, they also have things that are working just as they are. Even the most disastrous of rooms contain some systems that make sense. That's why the next step in organizing your room is to take an inventory —not just of what you want to change, but what you *don't* want to change.

To get started, spend a few minutes identifying at least 3 to 5 things, however small, that *are* working right now in your current setup. See the examples below.

What Works

- Magazines fit well in my bedside bin for late-night reading.
- I can always find the CD I'm looking for.
- All my workout clothes are in one place —it's easy to grab them and go for a run.
- The T-shirt drawer stays relatively neat.
- My comfy chair is right by the window, so it's a sunny place to read.

Your turn:

What Works

- _____
- _____
- _____
- _____
- _____

Next, make a **Fix List** by writing down at least five things that don't seem to be going as well—even if you have no idea right now how to fix them. We've come up with this sample list.

Fix List

- For some reason I am always missing just one shoe.
- I want to do yoga every day, but my floor is too cluttered.
- I don't know what to do with that stack of video games near the wall.
- I am constantly being hounded to clean my room.
- I can never find a pen in that drawer.
- There's no place to put my gloves and scarves.

Your turn:

Fix List

- _____
- _____
- _____
- _____
- _____

These two lists provide valuable clues as to why some things work better than others. Look again at what's working well and try to see why. Is the placement convenient, the storage the right size, the accessibility simple? Now look at the items on your Fix List. What's not working? And why not? As you read on, your mission will be to solve these problems and to make your room —without doubt—your favorite place to be.

Easy Fixes

Odds are many of the problems on your **Fix List** are just about misplacement, meaning that some of your items have the wrong home. Even your best stuff is useless if you can't get to it when you need it. Here are two major tips for organizing the stuff in your room.

Fix #1: Keep It Together

To make it simple to find what you need, keep items of the same kind in the same place. Hang all your belts in one spot, store shirts and jeans in separate drawers, and put CDs with DVDs and other media stuff. Or if there's another way to sort things that makes more sense to you—like organizing clothes by color, season, or where you wear them—cook up your own system instead. The idea is to let you see all the options for a certain thing at once so that choosing what you want will be quick and easy.

Fix #2: Location Is Everything

As you decide where each thing will go, consider how often you use it. If there's something that you need every day (like your cell phone or the baseball hat you take off only to shower and sleep), make sure to assign it a place front-and-center so it's easy to find and easy to reach. Likewise, don't waste prime real estate on your old talent show costume from 6th grade. For the stuff you use less often, like the blue feather boa you only wear on Halloween, choose a lower-profile spot farther off the beaten path: the attic, a closet shelf, or an out-of-the-way drawer.

Free Floaters

Even more frustrating than misplaced stuff is the stuff that has no place at all. These homeless items—also known as **Free Floaters**—can be tricky to spot. Sometimes an item has been sitting in one place for so long, you don't even notice it anymore. (That dusty pile of magazines you've been stepping over for six months, for instance.) And even if you do finally notice it, it's tempting to just leave it there. Tempting, but not a good choice. Every item needs a home, and if you never actually assigned it one, it's probably still homeless.

 **GIVING THINGS A GOOD HOME**

The Problem

Your parents think that the reason you do your homework on the floor is because you like it. Are they kidding? The floor is HARD. The truth is, your desktop is so crammed with school stuff that you have no other choice. Every book, every graded test, and every pen you own just always ends up there. Your parents keep hounding you to "put it all away." Your response: "Yeah, OK, but exactly where is away?"

Bottom Line

You've got a restless army of things eating up your space. Homeless and doomed to roam your room in a state of perpetual limbo, these **Free Floaters** get shuffled from place to place but never actually get put away. You can solve the problem by assigning every school item a permanent home in shelves, drawers, and labeled file boxes. The only things left on your desk should be your computer, pens, and a lighting source. (And your forehead, of course, when you're doing geometry.).

What To Do

Walk around your room and notice what school stuff is where. As you go, ask yourself: Where would be a good home for this? Decide on a place and then assign the object a new home.

3 Use It or Lose It
What to keep and—yes—what to toss

So, now you've got some ideas about how to reorganize. But none of it will work if you're still saddled with too much stuff.

Whether it's an insanely soft T-shirt or a series of funny snapshots, the possessions you love can add a lot to your life. But when the act of acquiring things becomes an end in and of itself, it's easy to wake up and find you've become a slave to stuff. If clutter is compromising your quality of life, you have two choices: Move some stuff out, or move into the garage with the cat's poop box. If litter box living appeals to you, feel free to stop reading now and go pack. But if you're ready to reclaim your room, schedule a **Clean Sweep Saturday**.

As the name suggests, Clean Sweep Saturday is a day devoted to sorting through one's cherished belongings (aka one's junk). This is the moment of truth, when you decide what to keep and what to toss. Don't worry if you don't finish sorting through your whole room in one day. For maximum impact, focus on one small section at a time, starting with the most noticeable areas first. This way your hard work will have an instant effect on your life. And if you need some extra motivation, revisit the room map you made on page 74 to remember what it is you are making space for.

Here's what you'll need:

- 3-5 large cardboard boxes
- permanent marker
- trash bags
- music
- power snacks

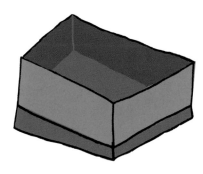

Room Dump

Empty out the contents of one section of your room so that everything's lined up on the floor or your bed. From there, sort your belongings into four groups.

Group #1: Stuff to Keep

Includes: Items you really love, things you use regularly, and anything you *know* you'll need in the future, even those orange fuzzy slippers and tattered old baseball caps—as long as you still use them.

Group #2: Stuff to Toss

Includes: Items that are broken, seriously damaged, or otherwise unusable. Your broken pink ruffle umbrella from the 5th grade? That goes here.

Group #3: Stuff to Give Away

Includes: Anything that could be useful to someone else but that you haven't used, looked at, or thought about in a year. This includes old clothes, CDs, books, and those knee-high rubber boots you wore in *The Pirates of Penzance*. To give yourself some extra incentive here, pick a worthwhile cause that's meaningful to you—a local religious organization that helps the needy, a homeless shelter, or any other reputable group that takes donations—and passes your stuff on to others. Some organizations will even come to your house to pick it all up, making it both fulfilling *and* easy to give stuff away.

Group #4: The Doubt Box

To bridge the gap between treasure and trash, use a **Doubt Box**. This is the perfect destination for stuff you're not sure about. (Hmmm … will I ever wear this cut-off, puffy-painted tank top again?) Maybe you like it but haven't used it in a while, or maybe there's a chance you might need it some day. Whatever the dilemma, toss it in the Doubt Box if you're not sure. Once the box is full, tape it up, add today's date, and put it someplace hidden away, like your closet, attic, basement, garage, or any other little unused nook in your house. Make a note in your planner to go out and look through the stuff again in three months to see what you missed and what you didn't. This out-of-sight, out-of-mind technique usually makes it clear whether you want something or not. And if, at the end of three months, you find there's something you just can't live without, it will have officially earned its place in your room. (Though you might want to think twice about that tank top.)

The Secrets of Sorting Success

As you sort through your things, focus on each item's value to *you*, not its value to someone else. For example, get rid of the ink cartridge that cost $12 when you bought it but that fits only the printer you gave away last year.

When you find yourself questioning what to do with that foreign coin collection you've been stockpiling since you were eight, ask yourself:

- Do I love this?

- Can someone else get more use from this than I do?

- Which is worth more to me: this thing, or the space it's taking up in my room?

If making decisions is especially tough for you, get a friend to help. You can lure him or her with the promise of first dibs on anything you don't want, or do an organizing swap (spend one day on your room and the next day on your friend's). It's always good to have someone there to reassure you that, yes, your old purple-glitter ice skating outfit is scary, and it's definitely time to toss it.

ORGANIZATION INSPIRATION

Having trouble getting motivated for a **Clean Sweep Saturday?** Try these ideas:

- Invite a friend over to keep you company (and make snack runs) while you are sorting.
- Blast your stereo with your favorite CDs (your parents will be too happy you're cleaning to complain).
- Think of it as a time to stroll down memory lane and journal about what you find.
- Collect old scraps of memorabilia as you go and make a scrapbook with them later on.

4 Playing Favorites
Learn to be selective

Some people just really love … everything. So much so, in fact, that their rooms gradually morph into shrines to the clutter gods; even their *stuff* has stuff. If you find yourself hoarding movie stubs from two years ago or refusing to part with stuffed animals you never even liked, you know what we're talking about. But contrary to your deepest fears, "clearing stuff out" is not code for "getting rid of stuff you love." The point is to get rid of stuff you *don't* love.

If the thought of parting with *anything* makes your stomach do flip-flops, practice the art of prioritizing. Instead of deciding what needs to go, focus on what you want to keep.

Here's a three-step approach:

1. Empty all the contents of one area of your room onto the floor or bed, then rank them by importance beginning with your favorite things first. (The most important things get the highest rankings: 1, 2, 3.) Start to put each highly ranked item neatly back in its place.

2. When you run out of storage (and that means no cramming!), the lowest ranked items get packed into cardboard boxes. Don't panic—they're not going far: Just mark each box with the date and stack them someplace out of the way for now, knowing they'll be there if you want or need them.

3. Make a note in your planner to come back and look through these boxes again in three months.

This approach delivers the best of both worlds: Your things stay safe, *and* your room gets a makeover. But there's a hidden bonus, too. By the time three months are up, the stuff in the garage might not be as appealing. You might even be ready to donate a box or two to a local charity. Who knows, someone might actually want your old *Boyz 2 Men* sweatband. Doubtful, but possible.

TRY IT ▶ PRIORITIZE AND PACK AWAY

The Problem

You hit the jackpot at a yard sale today: five bucks for a huge box of amazing vintage clothes. When you get home, you realize there's absolutely no space left in your closet; it is officially packed. You love your clothes—no way are you parting with anything. So, the new stuff gets smooshed into a drawer or piled on the floor, where it quickly gets so wrinkled, trampled, and dusty that you don't even want to wear it.

Bottom Line

You're out of space. This leaves you with two choices: Increase your storage, or give something the heave-ho. You might not want to give anything up, but you can still rank your clothes by preference. By packing your least favorites and off-season gear away into boxes, you make some breathing room. Now there's enough space to hang the new clothes *and* enjoy the stuff you already had. (You might even uncover a few classics you'd missed and forgotten were there, like those patched-up cords and perfectly broken-in jeans.)

What To Do

Think of an area in your room that's always brimming with stuff, like your desktop. Now ask yourself what it might be like if you could use that space the way you want to (like actually being able to open a book on it). With that vision in your mind, prioritize your items in order of what matters to you most. Then add them back one by one, until the area contains a comfortable amount of stuff but is not *too* full. Anything that doesn't fit will just have to be put away or stored elsewhere.

5 Finishing Touches
Maintain your organizational groove

If you've made it this far, you deserve an award — or at least a break from organizing. You'll get that break in a minute, but first you need to finish the job.

You've carved out your space. You've streamlined your stuff. Now it's time to complete your vision — and keep your room in order for the long haul.

Follow the Map

Go back to the map you made on page 74. Using that as a guide, rearrange your room by putting each item in the **Space** where it belongs. (If you're not sure where something should go, just think about how and when you like to use it and assign it a home.)

Don't worry if your real room layout turns out to be different from the map — you should adjust the floor plan to make the most of your space. The point of the map isn't to create limits; it's to inspire you to use your room the way you *want* to, instead of only thinking about where things fit.

The Science of Storage

You'll notice that, after cleaning things out and moving other stuff around, you now need storage containers to put away what's left. This is really important because the right containers will keep your room in top shape. To figure out what kind of containers you need, list your new Spaces and the things (that aren't furniture) inside them. Below are two examples.

Space 1: Music Space

- CDs

- iPod

- stereo

- remote control and headphones

Space 2: Exercise Space

• free weights

• yoga mat

• ankle weights

• Pilates DVD

Once you have all your things written down (and *before* you hit the stores or flea markets), use a measuring tape to figure out exactly what size shelves, racks, boxes, drawers, baskets, bins, or other things you'll need to keep stuff organized and make the best use of your space. The containers you choose should depend on the type of stuff, how often you use it, and its size and shape. Some storage containers come in collections; these are good because they let you combine pieces to store the things you have now, and leave you the option to add more storage if you need it later.

W.O.W words of wisdom

STORAGE ON THE CHEAP

If you have a lot of stuff to store, buying containers to hold it all can get expensive. For smart storage that's light on your wallet (and easier on the environment), look around the house for stuff to transform into creative containers. Here are just a few ideas:

• Turn an old wicker basket into a magazine bin.
• Use a juice glass for makeup brushes.
• Organize art supplies in a silverware tray.
• Turn a wooden milk crate on its side and use it to hold CDs.

(SMiLE!)

The Monthly Room Roundup

Now your room is organized and looking just the way you like it. To make sure that it stays that way, schedule a monthly tune-up session to see where things are. This 30-minute date is your opportunity to spot any old patterns that might be popping up—and to nip any new clutter in the bud.

BEFORE YOU GO...

So here you are, at the moment of truth. You've had a taste of what getting organized can do for your life, and now comes the real trick: staying organized. After all, it's one thing to get it together, and it's quite another to keep it that way.

That's why we've assembled the handy little cheat sheets in the back of the book. They come complete with everything you need to stay on track. Post them in a central spot, and use them regularly to keep your schoolwork straight, your schedule smooth, and your stuff in check.

If you hit a snag or start reverting to your old ways, don't be discouraged. Just think back to how good it felt to be organized, then jump back in. As we said in the beginning, being organized is not about perfection; it's strictly a quality-of-life equation. The more organized you are, the more head space you'll have left to enjoy the world around you—and all the great stuff in it.

Samantha Moss is co-author of *InSPAration*, a book for teens on healthy living, and author of *Pottery Barn Flowers* and *Pottery Barn Photos*. She also edited the award-winning Pottery Barn Design Library, a series of 10 books filled with style ideas for the home. Samantha is based in Oakland, California, where she lives with her husband, Boyd, and a shy little dog named Belly. To see what she's up to, visit her online at www.samanthamoss.com.

Lesley Schwartz is a professional teen organizer, academic coach and tutor. She started working with teens 10 years ago as a social studies teacher in the Bay Area. For the past three years, Lesley has combined her experience as an educator with her organizational skills to help teach kids organization and time management skills. Additionally, she created a customized academic planner now being used in Bay Area schools. She holds a bachelor degree from Wellesley College and earned a teaching credential from Mills College. Lesley lives in San Francisco, California. Visit her website at www.studentorganizationsolutions.com.

Michael Wertz has been a commercial artist since 1995. Since then, he has created work for *The New Yorker*, the de Young Museum, and the San Francisco International Film Festival. He lives in Oakland with husband Andy and dog Olive. You can see more of his work at www.wertzateria.com.

THE RIGHT SORT

The Three-Ring Binder and The Accordion File
WHAT GOES WHERE?

TAB #1
TO DO

To Do

- homework assignments

- homework calendars

- readings or worksheets you start in class but need to finish later

- directions for projects or papers to be done

- test study sheets

Put all stuff here until it is done. Then, once you finish any assignment, either hand it in or move it to **Current Topic.**

TAB #2
CURRENT TOPIC

Current Topic

- class notes

- notes on reading you've done outside of class

- articles or printouts related to topic

- completed worksheets

- graded homework assignments

Papers in this section should be stored in date order (date all of your notes and handouts). When you move onto the next topic in class, move the old papers from **Current Topic** into **Past Topics.**

TAB #3
PAST TOPICS

- everything from Current Topic, once that topic is completed

- returned tests, papers, and quizzes from old topics

Past Topics

When you move onto a new section in class, all the materials from **Current Topic** get moved here. As they come in, put them at the back of the section so that all of your papers are still organized by date.

TAB #4
REFERENCE

- course syllabus

- participation rubric

- information sheets (such as "how-to" sheets)

- reading lists

- reference sheets (such as the periodic table)

Reference

The order of these materials doesn't matter much, since there are usually not too many class reference materials. As long as they're handy, you'll be in good shape.

BACKPACK CHECKLIST

THE GOODS	PACKED?
textbooks for each class	
binders, notebooks, or files for each class, including whatever assignments are due	
planner	
pens and pencils	
calculator	
gym clothes	
after-school activity equipment and sports gear	
wallet	
ID/bus pass	
keys	
cell phone	
water bottle	
USB memory stick	

METHOD	DESCRIPTION	GOOD FOR BACKING UP FILES	GOOD FOR BRINGING ALONG
email	Send the document to yourself as an attachment.		✔
USB	Use a USB memory stick, which lets you save files in one place and then transfer them to your own hard drive later.	✔	✔
free online storage	Sign up with an online server like savefile.com or box.net, which will let you drag and drop files to store on the Web for free.	✔	✔
iPod	Attach an iPod or other MP3 player to your computer, and then drag and drop files onto it.		✔
external hard drive	Use this handy little gizmo to save everything on your computer's internal hard drive.	✔	
CD	When using CDs, burn a disk and then label it clearly with whatever's on it.	✔	✔

Week of_____

MONDAY   due date
- ❏ _____
- ❏ _____
- ❏ _____
- ❏ _____
- ❏ _____

After School _____

TUESDAY   due date
- ❏ _____
- ❏ _____
- ❏ _____
- ❏ _____
- ❏ _____

After School _____

WEDNESDAY   due date
- ❏ _____
- ❏ _____
- ❏ _____
- ❏ _____
- ❏ _____

After School _____

THURSDAY   due date
- ❏ _____
- ❏ _____
- ❏ _____
- ❏ _____
- ❏ _____

After School _____

FRIDAY   due date
- ❏ _____
- ❏ _____
- ❏ _____
- ❏ _____
- ❏ _____

After School _____

SATURDAY
_____
_____

SUNDAY
_____
_____

Upcoming Projects & Tests
_____
_____
_____
_____

Class Tracker®

Making your planner

1. Count

Check how many weeks are in your school year.

2. Copy

Photocopy the planner on the front of this card at 130%, then make enough copies for each week in your school year.

3. Bind

Three-hole punch your planner and put it into a three-ring binder, or have it bound by your local copy store.